My Hospital Book

My Hospital Book

William L. Coleman

BETHANY HOUSE PUBLISHERS
Minneapolis, Minnesota 55438
A Division of Bethany Fellowship, Inc.

All Scripture quotations are taken from *The Living Bible,* Copyright © 1971 by Tyndale House Publishers. Used by permission.

Copyright © 1981
William L. Coleman
All rights reserved

Published by Bethany House Publishers
A division of Bethany Fellowship, Inc.
6820 Auto Club Road, Minneapolis, Minnesota 55438

Printed in the United States of America

Library of Congress Cataloging in Publication Data

Coleman, William L.
   My hospital book.

   Summary: Text, suggested activities and pertinent Bible verses help acquaint the young patient with hospital operations and the duties of staff members.
     1. Hospitals—Juvenile literature.
     2. Children—Hospital care—Juvenile literature.
[1. Hospitals. 2. Medical care. 3. Christian life]
    I. Title.
RA963.5.C64   362.1'1   81–10094
ISBN 0-87123-354-1   AACR2

This book is presented to _____

by _____

on _____

Name of Hospital _____

Biographical Sketch

WILLIAM L. COLEMAN is a graduate of the Washington Bible College in Washington, D.C., and Grace Theological Seminary in Winona Lake, Indiana.

He has pastored three churches: a Baptist church in Michigan, a Mennonite church in Kansas and an Evangelical Free Church in Aurora, Nebraska. He is a Staley Foundation lecturer.

The author of 75 magazine articles, his by-line has appeared in *Christianity Today, Eternity, Good News Broadcaster, Campus Life, Moody Monthly, Evangelical Beacon,* and *The Christian Reader.* This is Coleman's twelfth children's book.

When you have to stay in a hospital for an illness or surgery, you want time to pass quickly, and you want to not be afraid. This book will help you in both ways. It will also help you learn some things you didn't know about hospitals, so that some day perhaps you might like to come back—as a nurse or doctor instead of as a patient.

John C. Wilcox, M.D.

Contents

- 13 • Going to the Hospital
- 15 • A Room Filled with Love
- 17 • Checklist
- 18 • My Room
- 21 • Will I Be Alone?
- 22 • My Family
- 23 • The First Night
- 25 • A Children's Doctor
- 29 • Nurses Are the Nicest People
- 31 • Sphygmomanometer Is a Great Tongue-Twister
- 33 • Bring Something from Home
- 35 • Draw a Map of Your Floor
- 37 • Time to Eat
- 38 • Can You Find It?
- 39 • Is It All Right to Cry?
- 41 • The Day of Your Operation
- 43 • My Operation Day
- 45 • The Operating Room
- 49 • Your Surgeon—The Man in the Funny Pajamas
- 51 • Your Surgeon's Tools
- 55 • Wake-Up Time—The Recovery Room
- 57 • Needles...Ugh!
- 61 • The Muscle Man
- 63 • Hospital Ministers
- 67 • Taking Pictures of Your Insides
- 71 • Bottles Hanging from Trees
- 73 • Keep Out
- 75 • Broken Bones
- 77 • Mixed-Up Medical Words

79 • Good-bye, Tonsils; Hello, Ice Cream!
81 • There Goes Your Appendix!
83 • How Did You Like Your Adventure?
84 • Autographs
93 • Summary of My Hospital Stay

How To Use This Book

It will make a terrific souvenir of your time in the hospital. Fill in the blanks, do the activities and keep a good record of your stay. Don't just sit back and wait to see what happens. Ask questions. Become involved. Make your hospital stay a great adventure.

Your time in the hospital can help mend your body. And during this time you can learn many new, exciting things. You can even learn more about the goodness of God.

Look through this book quickly and acquaint yourself with what is in it. At the back there are pages for autographs from the people you'll see in the hospital. Start collecting their autographs as soon as possible.

William L. Coleman
Aurora, Nebraska

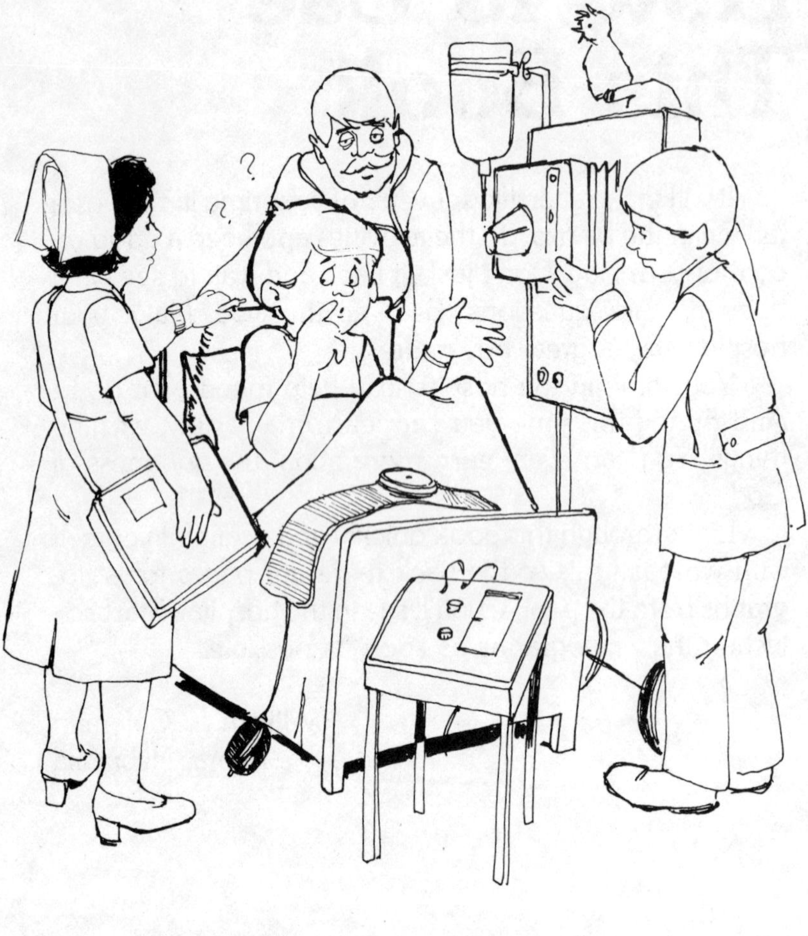

Going to the Hospital

While you are in the hospital, turn your stay into an adventure. It's like a trip to a mountaintop or a faraway jungle. You will learn things you never knew before. You will meet skilled doctors and nurses who can do amazing things for your body.

You will see machines, medicines, and gadgets you have never seen before. Be sure to ask questions. And when you learn something new, write it down so you can tell your friends about it.

You probably won't enjoy *everything* in the hospital. You might even get lonely. That's all right. Adults get lonely, too. Relax, learn, and let the doctors and nurses help you in *every way* they can.

Many people your age go to the hospital. One child out of ten will spend at least one night there this year. The average stay for your age group is four nights. Will your stay be longer or shorter than average?

Why are you going to the hospital? You will be surprised to learn how many different reasons there are. Some children are there for regular problems like having their tonsils taken out or having their appendix removed. A few have badly broken bones and need special work. You might meet a young person who is there just for tests. Some children are there for extra serious reasons. Maybe they are having trouble with their heart, kidneys or liver.

Why I am going to the hospital: _____
_____

Cooperate with the doctors and nurses and be the best patient you can be. That's the quickest way to be healthy again.

"Dear friend, I am praying that all is well with you and that your body is as healthy as I know your soul is" (3 John 2).

A Room Filled with Love

A hospital is a quiet place, but it's away from your home and your friends. As nice as a hospital room is, it isn't home. Most things that happen there will be new and strange. You will see dozens of people you have never met before. You will hear odd-sounding words which you won't understand. Lots of times you will wonder what those odd-looking machines are.

Nothing will happen in a hospital which you can't handle. Millions of children have been in hospitals before you. The doctors, nurses, and staff know what you are going through. They want to help you and send you home as soon as possible, so you can get back to your own clothes, enjoy your favorite foods, and see your friends again.

During those quiet nights when you are lying still, you might want to talk to someone. God is close by and He would like to hear from you. Tell Him how you feel. He wants to know what makes you happy. He also would like to know what frightens you. Tell Him what you need; God would like to help.

God lives in hospitals as well as anywhere else. You will feel a lot better if you talk to Him. While you are talking to God, ask Him to watch over your parents and grandparents. Ask Him to keep your brothers and sisters safe, too. Don't forget to pray for your doctors and nurses.

"Our fears for today, our worries about tomorrow, or where we are—high above the sky, or in the deepest ocean—nothing will ever be able to separate us from the love of God demonstrated by our Lord Jesus Christ when he died for us" (Rom. 8:38, 39).

Checklist

1. The date I came to the hospital: _____
2. The name of my hospital: _____
3. In what town or city is my hospital? _____
4. Who brought me to the hospital? _____
5. How long do I expect to be here? _____
6. What kind of vehicle brought me here? _____
7. What is my room number? _____
8. What was the weather like when I came into the hospital? _____
   _____
9. Have I stayed in the hospital before? _____ If so, when? _____
10. How would I describe the clothes I am now wearing?
    _____
    _____

My Room

1. What color is my room? _____ _____
2. Are there other patients in my room? _____ If so, how many? _____
3. How many windows are in my room? _____ What can I see through them? _____
4. Do I have a television set? _____ What kind? _____
5. Is there a table by my bed? _____ On which side of my bed? _____ What color is it? _____
6. How many chairs are near my bed? _____
7. Is there a crank to make my bed go up and down? _____ Where is the crank? _____
8. Is there a Bible in my room? _____ What color is it? _____
9. Does my room have curtains? _____ What color are they? _____
10. Is there a mirror in my room? _____

NURSE CALL
z-Buzz-zz-z
Bz-z-zz
NURSES TRACK RECORD
DISTANCE
TIME

Will I Be Alone?

One nice thing about a hospital is that you are never alone. Someone is always around.

How often will your parents be able to visit? Do you live far away or close by? Some parents rent a room near the hospital while their child is there. Some even rent rooms in the hospital and sleep there.

Hospitals are happy to have parents close to their children. Brothers, sisters, and friends may be another matter. Many hospitals have strict rules and won't allow anyone under 14 to visit patients; too many children walking the halls could get noisy. A few hospitals will let children in.

What are the visiting hours? _____
What ages can visit? _____
How many people may visit at once? _____

If you need someone in a hurry, your hospital has a special plan. Someplace near your bed there is an emergency button. Ask the nurse to show you where it is and explain how to use it. When you need help, merely push the button and someone will soon arrive to help you.

Where is my emergency button? _____

My Family

1. Do I have brothers or sisters? _____ Their names and ages: _____

   _____

2. Which members of my family have been in the hospital? _____

3. What are my parents' names? _____

4. Where do my grandparents live? _____

5. Do I have uncles and aunts? _____ How many can I name? _____

6. What kind of work do my parents do? _____

   _____

7. What do I enjoy doing with my parents? _____

   _____

8. What is my address? _____

9. What is my telephone number? _____

10. How far is my home from the hospital? _____

11. What color is my house? _____

12. Do I have pets? _____ What are their names? _____ Describe them. _____

13. What will be one of the first things I will do when I get home? _____

The First Night

What can you expect on your first night in the hospital? If you are in the hospital for surgery, your operation is probably scheduled for the next morning.

Most scheduled surgeries are done early on the next day after you enter the hospital. "Scheduled" means you had time to set a date for it. "Emergency" surgery has to be done immediately.

What you eat for dinner will depend on what kind of surgery you are to have. You might get only a bowl of soup. Many children eat a full meal, complete with dessert. What do you think will be on your plate for dinner?

Every hospital has a "lights out" time. If you have a television set, they will have to turn that off, too. What time do your lights have to go out? _____

Some time during the day or evening, the doctor who will operate on you will come in to see you. Make sure you record his name correctly: _____ .

The doctor stops by to check on you and tell you that everything is ready. This is a special chance for you to ask any questions you have. What questions will you ask? ____
_____
_____
_____

At bedtime you might receive a mild sleeping pill or other medicine. This will help you get a good night's sleep before the operation.

Around 11 o'clock at night different nurses will come to the hospital. The new nurse will be told all about your condition when she comes to work. If you should need her during the night, she will be close by.

A Children's Doctor

Ask your doctor if he is a pediatrician. If the doctor says yes, he is a special children's doctor. It means he had regular doctor training plus extra practice in taking care of young people such as yourself.

Also ask if you are in the pediatric section or ward. Most hospitals have such an area where only children are taken care of.

Usually children up to 12 years of age stay in the pediatric section. This section may have bright colors, pictures, toys and books. There also might be six or more beds in one large room. Large cities have entire hospitals filled with only children.

If you are in a large room in the pediatric ward, there might be a huge glass wall at the end of the room. This glass allows the doctors and nurses to see in as they walk past.

Many children enjoy having their own special section of the hospital. They can meet young people their own age, make new friends, and talk about the same things. All of this makes the time go faster.

When the doctors, nurses, and staff have time, ask them to help you answer these questions:

Is my doctor a pediatrician? _____
If not, what is my doctor's title? (Family doctor, surgeon, etc.) _____

Am I in a pediatric section of the hospital?_____ Does it have a special name?_____ Are there other children in my room?_____ What are their names? _____
_____
Is there a glass wall in my room? _____

"Then he placed a little child among them; and taking the child in his arms he said to them, 'Anyone who welcomes a little child like this in my name is welcoming me, and anyone who welcomes me is welcoming my Father who sent me!'" (Mark 9:36, 37).

Nurses Are the Nicest People

Some of the nicest people you will meet in the hospital will be nurses. They will take care of your daily medical needs and carry out the doctors' orders.

Some nurses wear a pin on their cap or on their uniform. This pin tells if they are an R.N. (Registered Nurse) or an L.P.N. (Licensed Practical Nurse). The pins have special designs on them to show which nursing school they attended.

You will have at least three nurses. Each will work for eight hours and then another one will come on duty. On the weekends you will probably get to meet even more nurses.

Get to know your nurses. They are your friends, and they will help you get well sooner.

Write their names down so you won't forget.

My Nurses	**Check One**	**Time of Work**
1. _____	R.N.__	_____
	L.P.N.__	
2. _____	R.N.__	_____
	L.P.N.__	
3. _____	R.N.__	_____
	L.P.N.__	
4. _____	R.N.__	_____
	L.P.N.__	
5. _____	R.N.__	_____
	L.P.N.__	

Nurse's aides help the regular nurses. Tell them your name and write their names down.

My Nurse's Aides   **Time of Work**

1. _____   _____

2. _____   _____

3. _____   _____

4. _____   _____

5. _____   _____

One of the most important things a nurse will do is check your "vital signs." They are called vital because they are very important clues to your health.

Each time a nurse comes on duty she will probably check your vital signs again. Ask the nure to tell you what your signs are the first few times and write down what she says.

My Vital Signs   1   2   3   4   5

1. Temperature   ___ ___ ___ ___ ___
2. Pulse (heartbeats per minute)   ___ ___ ___ ___ ___
3. Respiration (breaths per minute)   ___ ___ ___ ___ ___
4. Blood pressure   ___ ___ ___ ___ ___

Sphygmomanometer Is a Great Tongue-Twister

When the nurse checks your blood pressure, she will place a rubber tube around your arm. The real name of this gadget is *sphygmomanometer.* If you practice, by the time you can go home you will be able to pronounce this. Try it: sfig-mo-mah-nom'eter. See if the nurse can pronounce it for you.

Once the tube is placed on your arm, she will pump it up like a bicycle tire while she listens with a stethoscope. It will become tight on your arm. She will then let the air out and allow your blood to flow again.

Your nurse doesn't do this to find out how often your heart beats. She wants to know how *hard* it beats. She wants to know if it is pushing the blood hard enough, or maybe pushing it too hard.

If the blood isn't being pushed at the right pressure, the doctor may want to do something about it; but if he thinks it's safe, he will just leave it alone.

When blood pressure gets too high a blood vessel could break and cause terrible damage to the body. If the doctor knows this is a danger, he will control it with medicine. This problem doesn't usually affect children.

By now you are probably getting used to the hospital.

Keep learning. The more you know, the better you will enjoy your stay.

"We live within the shadow of the Almighty, sheltered by the God who is above all gods" (Ps. 91:1).

Bring Something from Home

Hospital rooms can be dull, though some hospitals try to liven them up with colorful walls or interesting pictures. Can you think of a few ways to make your room cheery? Maybe a couple of things from home would make you feel better.

Pictures are always nice to have around. How about a picture of your parents or brothers and sisters? If you have a photo of a close friend at school, put it on your table. When staff or visitors come in, tell them who the people are in your pictures.

Do you usually sleep with a stuffed animal? Many children do. If you left it at home, ask your parents to bring it. A soft, cuddly animal can remind you that you're not alone.

What about a good book? This could be the chance to read that special book. Most likely you will have hours to pass. Watching television is fun, but you might also enjoy a terrific sports book or an exciting adventure story.

Easy-to-hold games can make your stay seem shorter. Be careful not to bring noisy ones that might irritate other patients.

Your time in the hospital will be much more pleasant

if you take a few familiar things along. Your parents will be happy to bring something if you ask them. If you wonder whether it is allowed in the hospital, ask your nurse.

Draw a Map of Your Floor

How are the rooms in your hospital arranged? Where is the nurse's station? Is there a waiting room on your floor? Does your hospital have elevators or stairs?

Find out what is on your floor and then draw a picture. Ask people to describe the places you cannot see. When you have the facts together, you will be ready to make your map. Include as many details as you can.

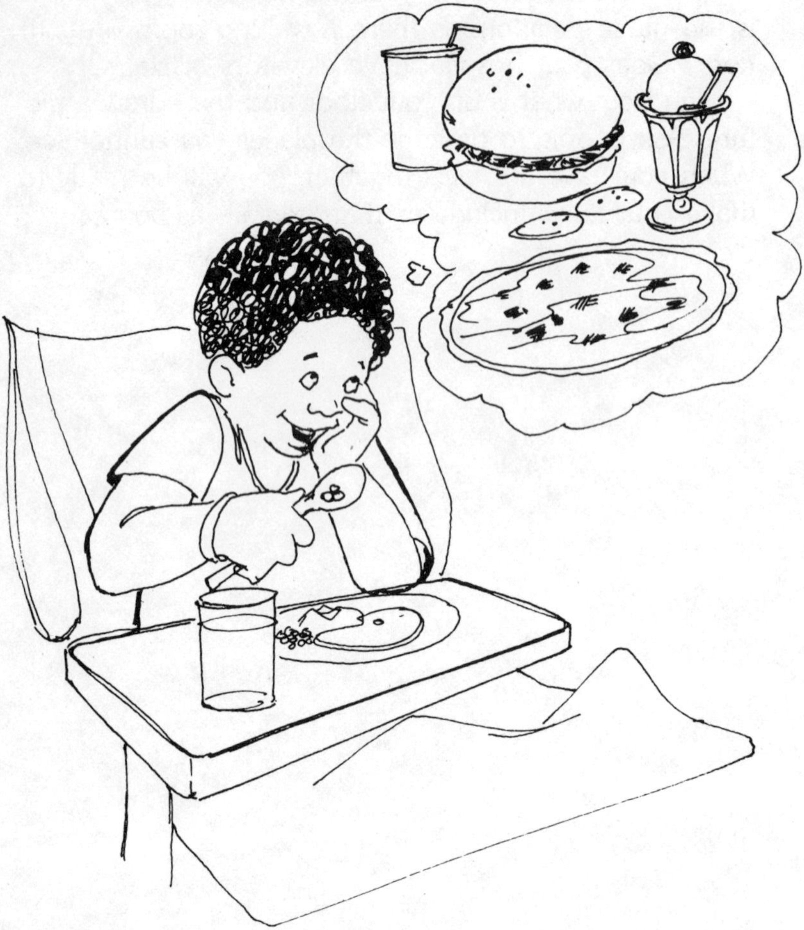

Time to Eat

1. Who brings my food?
   The person's name is: _____
2. What time do I eat?
   Breakfast _____
   Lunch _____
   Supper _____
3. Can I feed myself? _____ If not, who helps me?
   _____
4. One word that describes how I like the food:
   _____
5. What is the favorite food I have had so far in the hospital? _____
6. What is my favorite food at home? _____
7. Do I get food between meals? _____
8. Most of the time, I eat:
   ☐ a. all of my food   ☐ c. half of my food
   ☐ b. most of my food   ☐ d. a little
9. Are there some foods I am not allowed to eat? _____ What? _____
10. When I return home, what is the first thing I want to eat? _____

Can You Find It?

See how many places in the hospital you can find. If you can't find a few, ask someone.

1. The kitchen is near _____
2. The nurses' desk is near _____
3. Is there an elevator? _____ Where? _____
4. The nursery is near _____
5. Where is the nearest exit? _____
6. Where is the closest restroom? _____
7. The operating room is near _____
8. Where is intensive care? _____
9. Can you find the physical therapy room?_____ Where? _____
10. Where is the laundry room? _____
11. Where are X rays taken? _____
12. Is there a candy machine? _____ Where? _____

Is It All Right to Cry?

Yesterday I saw a football coach cry. He was big and strong but he didn't hold the tears back. No one thought he was a sissy because he cried.

Children often wonder if they should cry. They want to be brave and strong and they are afraid crying looks weak. But sometimes it's natural to cry. Maybe you have a pain in your side. Possibly your leg has ached all day and you can't stand it anymore. You may have a shot and the pain was awful. All of these things happen and they can make someone cry.

We have all seen silly crying. It's the spoiled kind. A child will throw a fit; he'll stomp his feet and scream and make a big scene. This person just wants his own way. This type of crying always looks bad.

No one has to be ashamed of crying when something really hurts. Often loneliness hurts as much as any pain. You wouldn't be the first person to cry on a pillow at night.

Men and women, boys and girls all know how to cry. Sometime you may need to cry in the hospital. That's all right. When it was necessary to cry, Jesus wept, too (John 11:35).

"What happiness there is for you who weep, for the time will come when you shall laugh with joy!" (Luke 6:21).

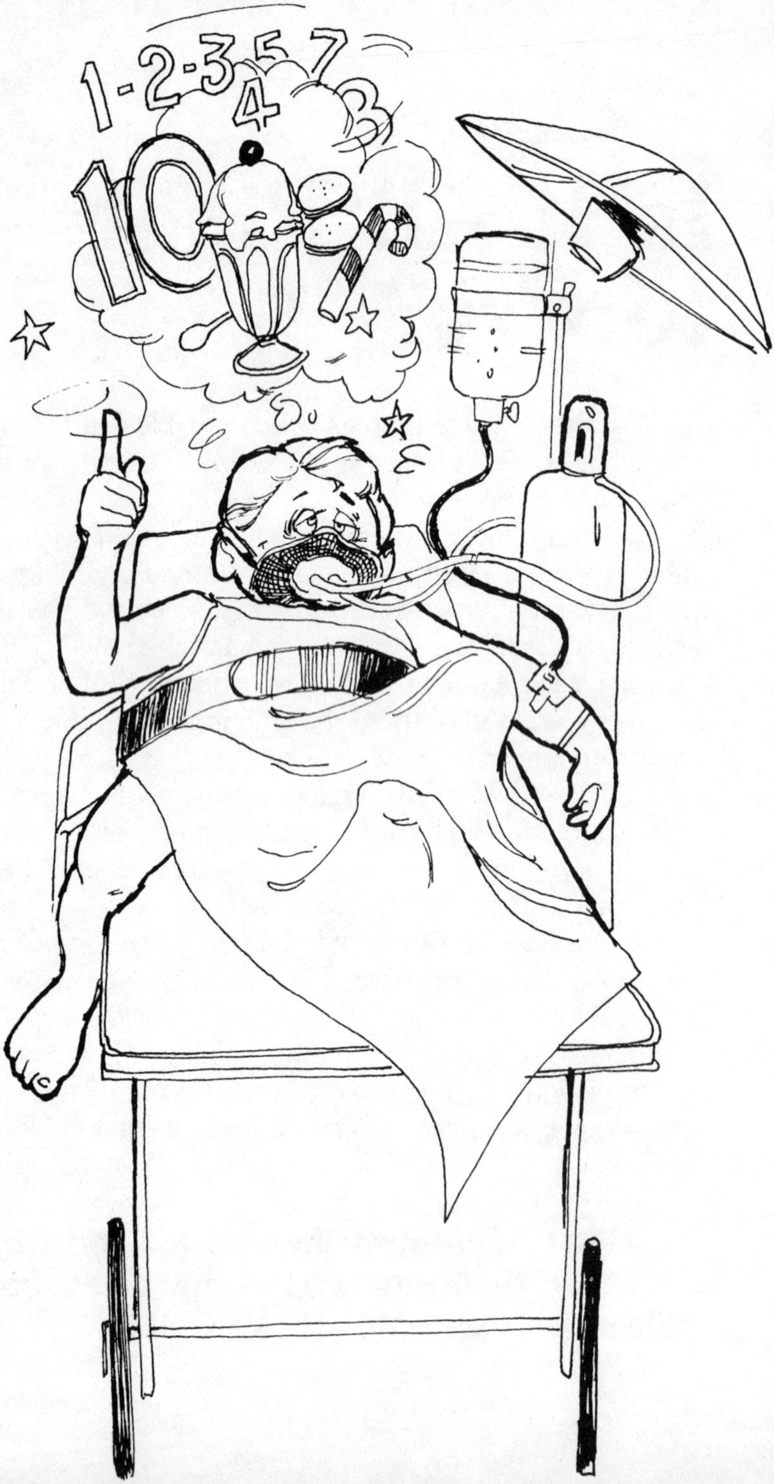
1-2-3
5 7
4
3
10

The Day of Your Operation

On the day of your operation many people will be working for you. They will start early in the morning. Their years of training will come in handy to make things go just right for you.

Generally, your operation will follow this schedule. After you have recovered, check to see if yours was different.

Surgery usually begins early, around 7:00 or 8:00 a.m., depending on how many people are scheduled that day.

Early in the morning the nurse will come in to check you. She will investigate your vital signs one more time. Then the nurse will give you a shot. This has a double purpose. First, it will calm you down and make it easier to put you to sleep later. Second, it will reduce the amount of saliva in your mouth (saliva is also called "secretions").

You probably won't be allowed to eat breakfast. This will prevent your stomach from being too full.

How will you get to the operating room? In some hospitals you might be rolled down the hall on your bed. In other places you will be moved to a special mobile bed. These have side rails and are specially designed for moving patients. It will be interesting to see how they move you down the hall.

When you are wheeled into the operating room, your bed will be pushed alongside the operating table. How you get from the bed to the table will depend on your condition. They might lift you from one to the other. If you are able, they'll probably just tell you to crawl over.

Lying on your back, you will be looking up into some large, bright lights. They might be a little hard to get used to, but they are a big help during the operation.

Some time during these activities you will want to pause and pray. You can do it with your eyes open if you want. Ask God to watch over you and guide the doctor's hands. The Holy Spirit can calm you down and get you ready for surgery.

After surgery fill out this checklist as well as you can. If necessary ask the staff to help.

My Operation Day

1. Who was the first person to come into my room the day of my operation? _____
2. How early did the nurse come in? _____
3. Did she check my vital signs? _____
4. Did I get a shot? _____
5. Was anyone from my family with me before my operation? _____
6. Who? _____
7. How was I moved to the operating room? _____
8. How did I get onto the operating table? _____
9. Did the lights hurt my eyes? _____

The Operating Room

When you go into the operating room, you may notice that it's cool. The nurses and doctors are dressed warmly and the lower temperature will make them feel more comfortable. This doesn't mean you will be cold, only cooler than you were in the hall. You won't feel this way for long because you will soon be asleep.

If you remember to look, notice the color of the operating room. It will probably be a soft white, blue, or green. These colors help cut down the glare from the powerful lights.

There will be two or three nurses in the room, all wearing masks to make sure you don't get germs. They will wear hoods covering their hair, because hair is difficult to get really clean, no matter how much it is scrubbed.

The person who puts you to sleep is an anesthetist (an-es'-the-tist). He gives anesthesia. Often he is a doctor who has two more years of special training. Sometimes it's a nurse with extra schooling.

By the time you have noticed all of this, the anesthetist will gently place a mask over your mouth and nose. You'll enjoy this. Some masks are shaped like space helmets. The mask will have tubes leading to tanks standing nearby. A gas to make you sleep comes through the tubes. Sometimes the gas may even smell like chocolate or butterscotch!

Often the anesthetist will talk to you and make you feel relaxed. He may then ask you to take a deep breath, or count to ten or backwards from 100. In just a few seconds you will be asleep.

Sometimes a patient will start to go to sleep, but he can feel cold instruments in his mouth or he can still hear people talking. One boy was afraid the surgeon would start the operation before he was completely asleep. This can't happen. You also can't wake up during the operation. The anesthetist will have total control, so just relax.

It isn't unusual to dream during surgery. Before you fall asleep, pick out the subject you want to dream about; maybe it's playing ball or mountain climbing. How about crossing the sea on a one-person boat? Start to think about it and see what happens.

Keep mental notes. Later answer these questions about the operating room.

My Surgery

1. What color was the operating room? _____
2. How many nurses were in the room? _____
3. What color were their clothes? _____
4. What did the gas in my mask smell like? _____
5. What type of gas was it?
   ☐ "laughing gas" (nitrous oxide)
   ☐ sodium pentothal
   ☐ ether
   ☐ cyclopropane
   ☐ other _____
6. What did the anesthetist ask me to do? _____
7. Did I dream during surgery?_____ What was the dream about? _____
   _____
8. Was the room cool? _____

"Then I lay down and slept in peace and woke up safely, for the Lord was watching over me" (Ps. 3:5).

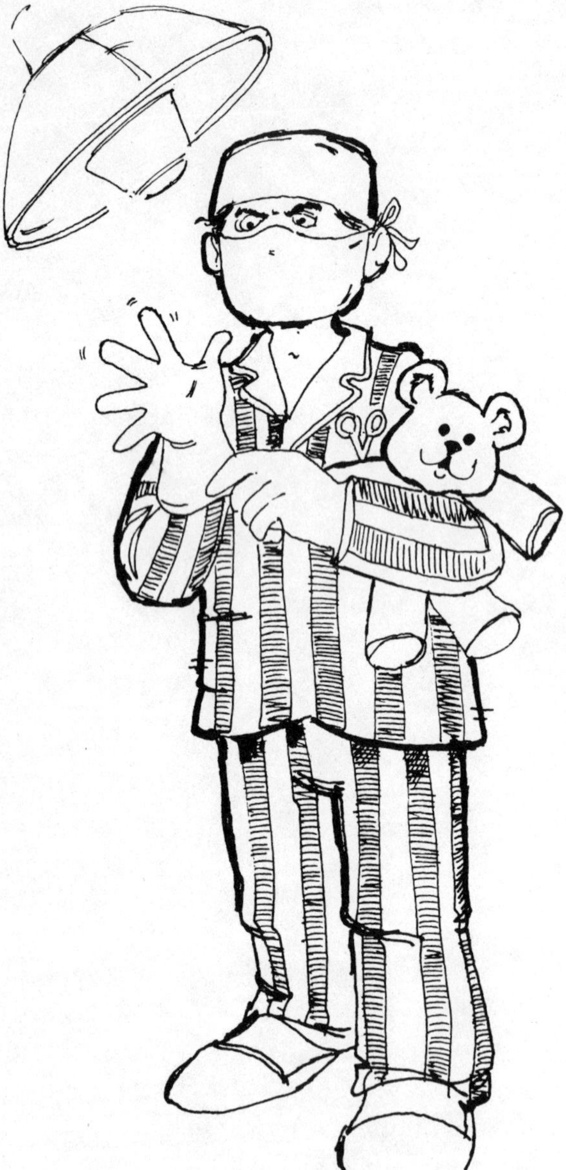

Your Surgeon — The Man in the Funny Pajamas

Before your operation the surgeon will come to your room and talk to you. The conversation may not be long, but at least you'll get to meet him. He may briefly describe your operation for you. If you have any questions, be sure to ask him. Then you won't have to go to surgery afraid of something you don't understand. Asking a couple of questions could clear up a lot of things.

You might not see the surgeon again until after the operation. Many times he doesn't enter the operating room until after the patient is asleep.

Maybe more than one doctor will operate on you. This depends on the type of surgery and where the hospital is located. A large city is likely to have more doctors available.

While you are preparing for surgery, your doctor is, too. He will put on a baggy shirt and pants that look like pajamas. They are usually green or blue. The doctor will also wear special shoes or shoe covers. A cap will keep his hair tucked in and a mask will cover his nose and mouth. All of this is carefully done to keep germs from getting into the operating room.

The surgeon will wash his hands with a germ-killing liquid soap. The sink he uses will have foot controls so he won't have to touch faucet handles. Then the doctor will dry his hands with sterilized towels. He is not to touch anything that hasn't been completely cleaned.

No part is more important than the gloves worn by the doctor. He doesn't put these on himself but has someone help him. Don't think of heavy cotton work gloves, but thin rubber ones. They are so thin that the surgeon can feel through them. Usually the gloves are a light tan color.

Now the doctor is ready. He will use his many years of training and experience to solve your problem.

Your Surgeon's Tools

You probably won't get to see them, but your surgeon will use some fascinating instruments during your operation. They have been selected and prepared with just your surgery in mind.

The day before your operation the stainless steel instruments will be laid out and prepared. They will be sterilized in a hot oven using high heat and steam. The instruments will be cooled so don't worry about getting burned. Each is double wrapped to keep it sterile (germ-free).

After the instruments are sterilized, no one can touch them unless wearing special gloves. Every precaution is taken to make sure they are completely clean for your surgery.

The instruments are then placed on a tray. The tray is put next to the operating table before your surgery begins.

A surgical assistant will hand the instruments to the doctor as he needs them. He calls out the name of the tool and the assistant hands it to him. After the operation they must be sterilized again before they can be used.

When the surgery is completed, your skin will be closed with stitches, often called "sutures." Stitches are strings sewn into the skin with a small curved needle.

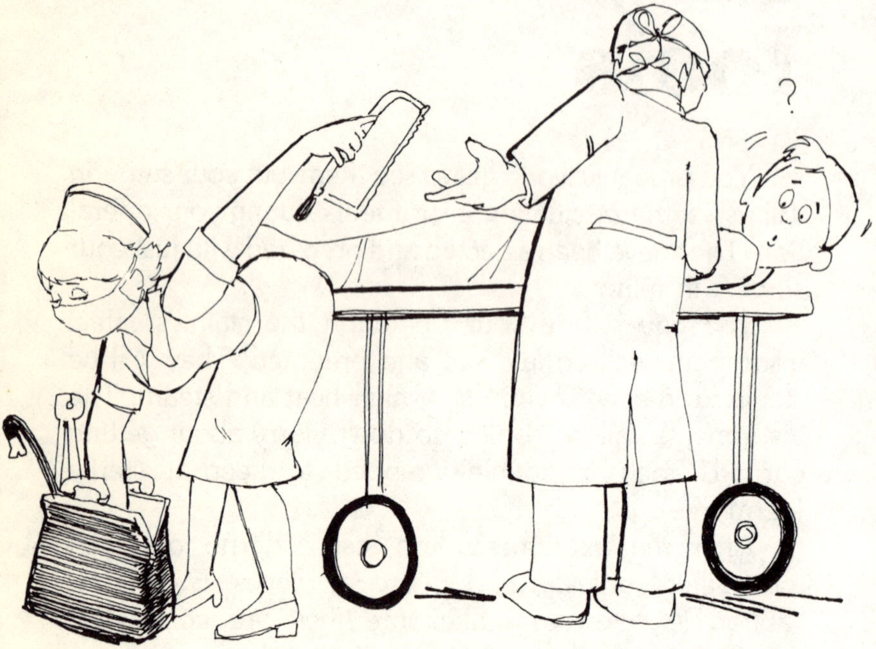

Stitches are not always used. Sometimes tight bandages will allow the opening to heal.

What kind of stitches will you have? If they are stitches inside your body (internal stitches), they will probably dissolve after they have done their job. Even if they don't dissolve, they should be no problem if left inside.

If you have stitches on the outside of your skin, they will have to be removed. The doctor will take them out in about a week. He will do this in his office. You will barely feel anything as he snips and removes them. This is an easy part after the operation.

By the time the stitches are taken out, you will be well on your way to recovery. You will have some great reasons to be grateful. You can be thankful for good doctors, modern medicine, loving parents and most of all, a caring God. Take time to be thankful.

Turn your memory up high and write down some more facts. Later you will enjoy reading this again.

1. Will my internal stitches dissolve? _____
2. How many stitches did I get on the outside? _____
3. When will these stitches be removed? _____
4. Will they be removed in the doctor's office or at the hospital? _____
5. If I didn't get stitches, how did they close me up? (Ask someone.) _____
6. What am I most thankful for right now? _____
   _____
7. Have you thanked anyone? _____ Who? _____

"Let [God] have all your worries and cares, for he is always thinking about you and watching everything that concerns you" (1 Pet. 5:7).

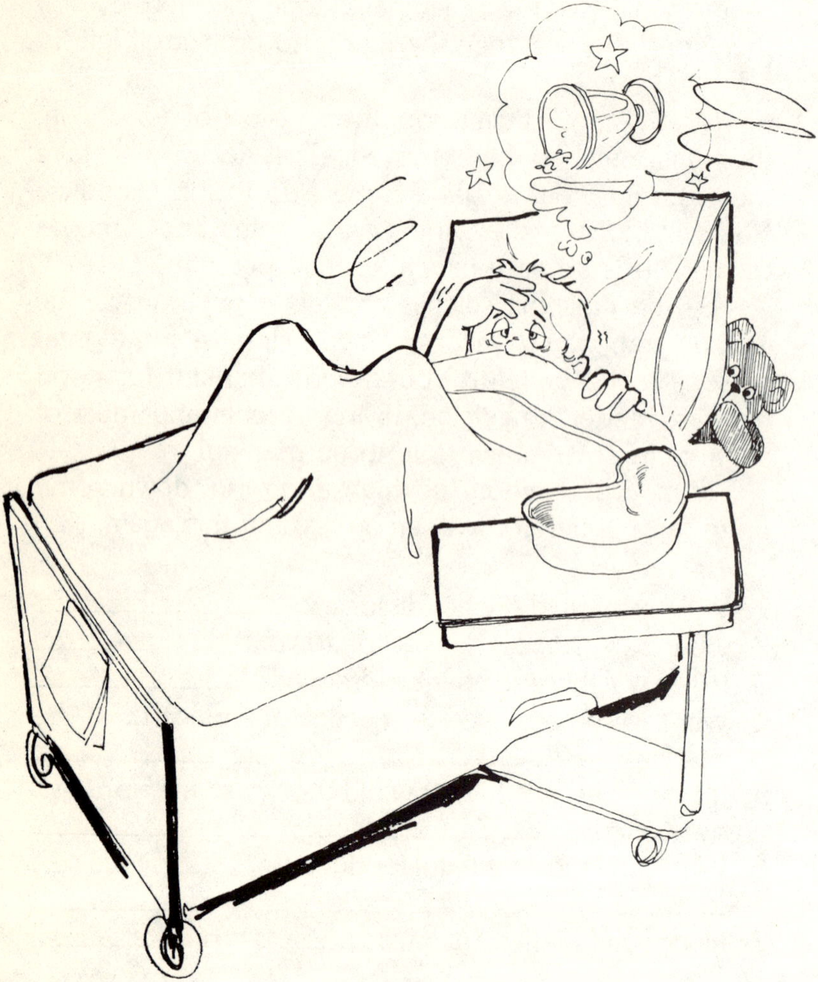

Wake-Up Time – The Recovery Room

Where will you go after your surgery? You can't stay in the operating room; the next patient will need that. When the operation is completed, you will be taken to a recovery room.

The recovery room can be confusing if you don't know what to expect. Most likely there will be other patients in the room. You will be a post-operative patient ("post" means after). When you begin to wake up, you will hear people talking. At first you may not be able to hear what they are saying. You might even think you are dreaming.

Don't be surprised if it sounds like everyone is talking too loudly. They are speaking normally. It's just the way you hear at first.

You might feel sick to your stomach. That's normal and the feeling will go away.

There are several things you can expect. Your arms and legs will feel like wet lumber—heavy and dull. You will have trouble focusing your eyes. Good sight will come back soon. The room might feel as cold as a refrigerator.

If you try to move, the spot where your surgery was

may be terribly sore. Don't panic. It won't be long before your body starts to calm down again.

The nurses will check all your vital signs—your pulse, body temperature and blood pressure—regularly. As soon as everything is fairly normal, they will return you to your regular room. Even though your surgery is finished, there is still much to do. The nurses will keep a close watch on you for some time to come.

Before the surgery:
1. Will I be in a recovery room? _____
2. Where is it located? _____
3. What color is the room? _____
4. Are the lights dull or bright? _____
5. How many people will the recovery room hold? _____
_____
6. How long do I expect to be there? _____

After the surgery:
1. When I woke up, what was the first thing I thought of?
_____
2. How did I feel when I woke up? _____
_____
_____

Needles . . . Ugh!

Most of us don't like getting "shots." Even adults often find it painful. Sometimes a needle can be quick and you will barely feel it. Other needles really hurt and can even make you cry. If you cry, everyone understands. It isn't fun to be hurt.

Shot, hypo (hypodermic), injection—they all usually mean the same thing. The tool for doing it usually has two parts: the fat tube which holds the medicine, called a syringe, and the short, pointed needle. With it, the doctor or nurse can either put something in you or take something out of you. Maybe the doctor will want to take a small amount of your blood and examine it.

Scientists are making more medicine into pills, so that needles won't have to be used so much. However, we aren't likely to get rid of needles completely.

Some time you might receive a shot from a "gun." This "shoots" the medicine into your arm with air pressure. It is very quick and it usually doesn't hurt much.

Many people are in good health today because they have had medicine from needles. Some would not be able to live normal lives if it were not for these pointed helpers.

Most of us get a shot sooner or later. Often the needles are shot into the arm. But don't be surprised if you have to lean over and receive a needle from behind.

You might also receive a needle just under your skin. In this case the medicine moves slowly into your body. Another time you could receive a needle into a muscle area; the medicine will move more rapidly. If the needle is placed into a vein, the medicine will move very quickly.

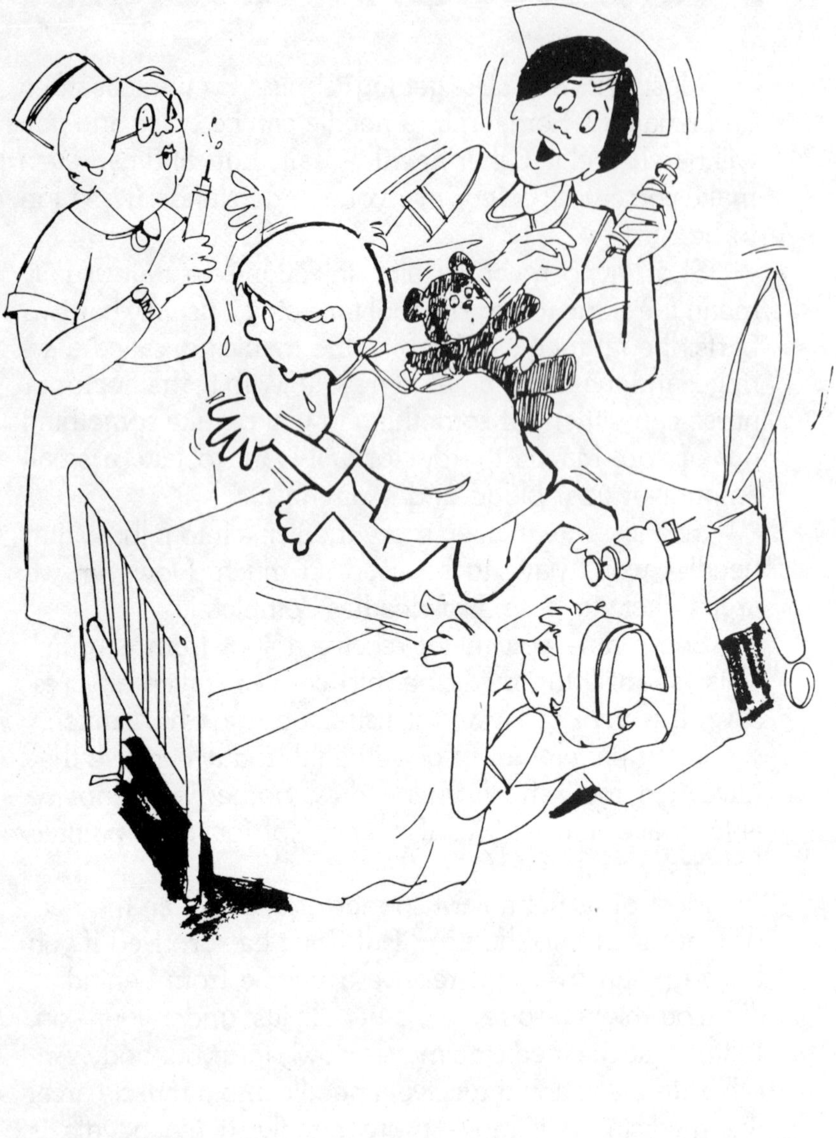

How many shots have I had in my life?_____
I will keep count. I will write down each day I receive a shot and what kind of shot it was.

_____
_____
_____
_____

"For I cried to him and he answered me! He freed me from all my fears" (Ps. 34:4).

The Muscle Man

There are a couple of fascinating people you should get to know. They aren't doctors, but they do a terrific job of helping patients. One person is the physical therapist (PT) and the other is the occupational therapist (OT). Both therapists are dedicated to getting the patient back to an active life as soon as possible.

The physical therapist is usually the muscle man. His job is to teach patients to use their muscles, limbs, crutches, canes, or walkers. This could mean learning a new way to walk or even to stand. It could mean strengthening important muscles in your arms.

A therapist has special training in body control. He can work for hours with a person and often make a big change in his life. If possible he gives the patient an exercise program which he can do at home.

If you need this therapist, he can make a big difference in your body. He may give you some treatment while you are in the hospital and then have you come back for more visits.

The occupational therapist (OT) can be just as important. His job is to make sure you can get along with your daily living. For instance, if you will need a wheelchair, how do you handle it? Will you be able to get out of the chair into your bed by yourself? He will show you how.

What if your arm is in a cast for a long time? How will you cut your own meat? The occupational therapist can show you this, too. Will someone else have to dress you? Not if the OT can teach you another way. How will you go to the bathroom? The OT will probably show you how. He can provide all sorts of methods and equipment to help patients get back to normal.

If you need a therapist, there are many hours of hard work ahead. However, they are helpful, interesting hours. Therapists are a gigantic help.

1. Does my hospital have a physical therapist? _____
2. Does my hospital have an occupational therapist? _____
3. Will I need one of these therapists? _____ Why? __
   _____
   _____

4. Describe what a physical therapist does. _____
   _____
   _____

5. Describe what an occupational therapist does. _____
   _____
   _____

Hospital Ministers

If you are in the hospital for very long, you might get a visit from a minister. He is a friendly person and cares about people. He probably won't stay long, because he'll have several people to visit.

Many times a patient's pastor will come, but ministers are busy and sometimes forget someone in the hospital. If you want to make sure your pastor comes to see you, ask your parents to give him a call.

Your hospital might have a chaplain. A chaplain is a hospital minister. Some chaplains work full time for the hospital. Others pastor churches but are at the hospital part of the time. If you would like to visit with a chaplain, simply tell a nurse.

Make good use of the minister or chaplain. If you want to, he will talk a little about baseball or television. Ministers are also excellent at answering questions and discussing problems; and they are fantastic listeners.

Another good thing about ministers is that they are great secret-keepers. Do you want to tell someone something that you don't want others to know? Just tell the minister that it is top secret.

Anyone can pray for you and several people probably do. A minister would like to pray for you, too. Tell him how you feel. If something bothers you about the hospital or your operation, let him know. If there is anything else on your mind, you can say so. The minister can talk to God about it. He can ask Jesus to watch over you, protect

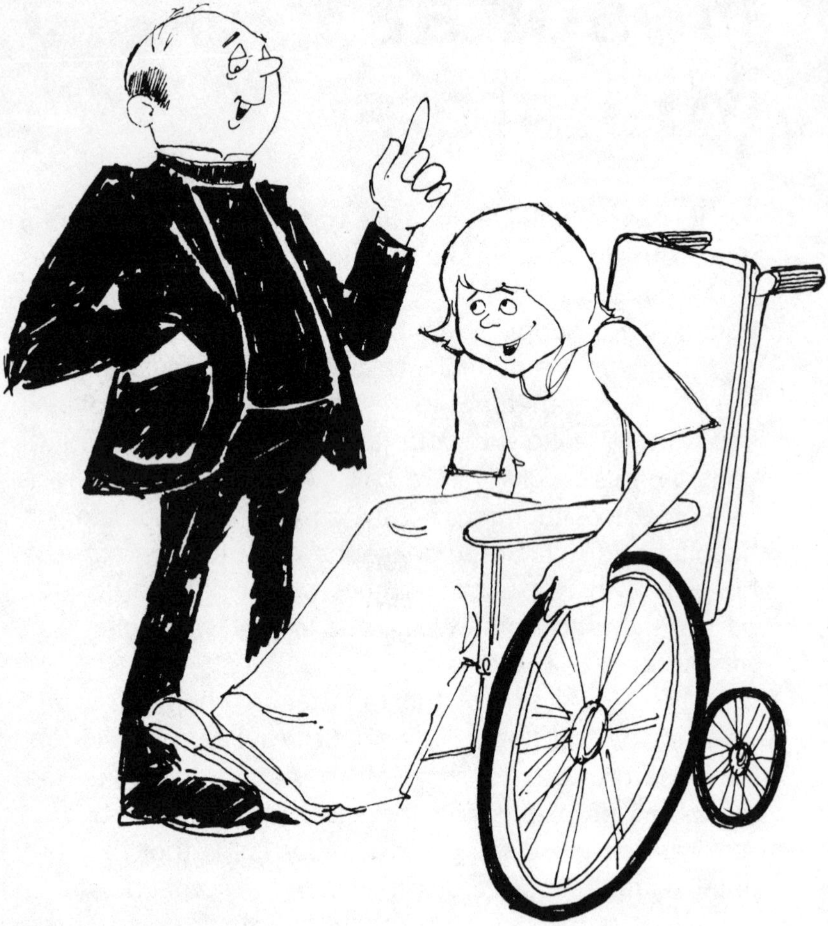

you and take away your worry.

If you want the minister to stop in again, make sure you tell him.

1. Has a minister or chaplain been to see me? _____
2. What is my minister's or chaplain's name? _____
3. How would I describe his appearance? _____
   _____
4. Did he pray with me? _____
5. Was he from my church, another minister, or working at the hospital? _____

"In the same way, everyone knows how much good some pastors do, but sometimes their good deeds aren't known until long afterward" (1 Tim. 5:25).

Taking Pictures of Your Insides

What do you look like on the inside? Would you like a picture of your ribs or knee joint, or a good view of your jawbone? It's easy for doctors to get these pictures with an X-ray machine.

Most of us will have X-ray pictures taken at some time. Before X-ray machines, doctors had to operate and then look around inside. Today they know what you look like inside *before* an operation, so that sometimes they don't have to operate at all.

X rays can be dangerous if too many are taken, but this isn't usually a problem to the patient. However, X-ray technicians (the people who operate the machines) who are around the machines all the time need to protect themselves, so they "duck out" while the picture is taken. Under normal use the X ray is safe for patients.

These machines are great for taking pictures of bones. However, they don't show our flesh and organs very well. If the doctor wants a picture of a stomach or intestine, he gives the patient a special liquid to drink. Then these parts will stand out clearly on the X-ray image.

A new, huge X-ray machine is being used in many large hospitals. It is called a CAT scanner. Not only is it big, but also very expensive. This machine is half X ray and half computer. It figures out what is going on in your body and reports it in three dimensions.

When the doctor reports the results of your X-ray pictures, you will need to pay attention. If he says the results

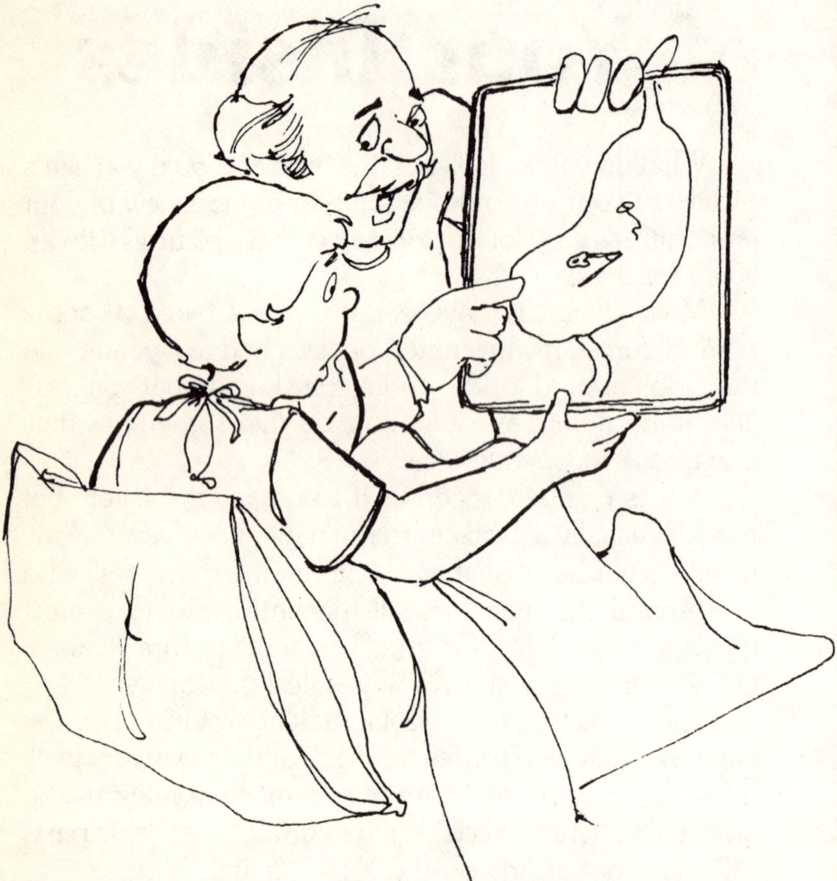

are "negative," that's great, but if the report is "positive," your body will probably need help. In a doctor's report "negative" is good, "positive" means something is wrong.

When you visit your doctor, ask him if he has any X rays of you. If he does, ask to see one. You will be amazed when you see how your body is put together.

See how much information you can find out about X-ray machines.

1. Where are the X-ray machines in my hospital?_____
   _____
2. Does my hospital have a CAT scanner?_____ Where is it kept? _____
3. Have I ever had X rays taken?_____ How many times? _____
   Did I stand up or lie down for my X rays? _____
4. Have I seen X rays of my body? _____
5. Did the doctor say my X rays were negative or positive? _____
6. Did my X-ray technician stay in the room or leave while the pictures were being taken?_____
7. What color was the X-ray machine?_____

Bottles Hanging from Trees

They look just a little like fake palm trees. The metal pole is on wheels and a bottle hangs from its arm like tropical fruit. They "grow" all around the hospital next to patient's beds. These are called intravenous bottles and are extremely important. They allow liquids to go into a patients's body when they have a hard time swallowing, or when he needs extra medicine.

Maybe this will never happen to you, but let's pretend. Suppose you have a condition that makes you throw up when you eat, or you have trouble staying awake. Maybe you've had serious surgery on your stomach or intestines. Whatever the reason, the doctor orders a bottle to put liquids into you another way.

A plastic tube will run from the bottle to the patient's arm. The nurse will tie a tourniquet around the arm. Pressure from the tourniquet makes a vein swell up. A needle is then put into the vein. The tube from the bottle is connected to the needle.

Liquids from the bottle will flow down the plastic tube into the vein. Since the bottle is hung high in the "tree," the liquid will flow by gravity. The nurse will adjust the flow from the bottle so you will get the right amount of liquid into your body.

What is in those bottles? Sorry, no pop or chocolate milk. You can ask the nurse for those, but she won't give them intravenously.

There might be liquid vitamins or calories in the bottle

to give the patient strength. Medicines are also included if the doctor believes the patient needs them.

Intravenous feeding is a gigantic help for those who need it.

Most of us will not be patients too often, so we want to learn as much as we can while we are there. Look around and see what you can learn about intravenous bottles. Don't be afraid to ask questions.

1. Have I had an intravenous bottle?_____ Why or why not? _____
_____

2. What is put into the bottles? (Ask your nurse.) _____
_____

3. Keep count. How many bottles do I see hanging from "trees" while I'm in the hospital? _____

4. Super detective! If I can get close enough to a bottle, I'll count the number of drops leaving the bottle per minute. _____

5. Describe what a tourniquet does: _____
_____
_____

Keep Out

While you are in the hospital, you might see a sign on a door which reads "Isolation—Keep Out." That will probably get your curiosity up. You might wonder, "Does the person in that room have a foreign disease that could spread quickly?" or, "Are there germs in the room which could infect an entire city?"

Be careful not to let your imagination work too hard. It's possible that the person has a disease which could be caught. If this is the case, the patient is getting special attention. Gloves and masks are worn by everyone who enters the room. His laundry is cleaned separately from anyone else's. Everything possible is done to keep the germs from reaching others.

More often the problem is just the opposite; the doctors are afraid of what *our* germs would do to the person in the "isolation" room. His body or blood is not working correctly. Our germs could give that person's body a serious illness. Be sure you do not enter that room—for the good of the person inside.

If the "Isolation" sign is on the door, stay out. It is the only safe thing to do.

Broken Bones

Have you seen hospital patients with broken bones? They probably have large white casts on their legs or arms. If they are in the hospital because of a break it is usually a serious one.

A broken bone is called a "fracture."

Most fractures will heal themselves. If you break your arm, it will grow back together if the bone hasn't moved too much.

Our bones have a special glue called callus. Almost immediately this glue begins to fill in the cracks and the healing begins. Some people have cracked a rib and without going to a doctor the bone has mended. If the bone will heal itself, why go to the doctor? It's his job to make sure the break is in a position to mend *correctly*. You don't want a crooked finger or a twisted arm. If the bone is out of place, he will reset it and make sure it is straight.

The doctor will usually put a plaster cast around the bone. Casts prevent the bone from moving too much. Without the cast a sudden shake or turn could cause the healing bones to separate. This could be terribly painful.

Not every broken bone needs a cast. In some cases the doctor might merely put it in a sling or wrap the bone tightly.

A "compound" fracture means the broken bone has torn into or through the skin.

Usually it takes around six weeks for a bone to heal properly. In some cases the time will vary.

If a person is in the hospital for a broken bone, it is because there are probably some added problems. Maybe the location of the break makes bed care necessary. Possibly the fracture is so severe that the bone is crushed. It also could be that the callus is not working correctly.

If the break is especially bad, a steel pin is used to help hold the bone together. After the bone heals, the pin may be removed or it could be left inside forever.

Be a detective of broken bones. See what you can find out about fractures.

1. Do I have a broken bone? _____ Which one? ____
   _____
2. How many people with casts have I seen in the hospital? _____
3. Can I name one person besides myself who is in the hospital with a fracture? _____
4. Why did that person's fracture need hospital care?
   _____
5. How long does that person expect to be hospitalized?
   _____

Mixed-Up Medical Words

The letters have been jumbled up. Can you spell the words correctly?

1. runse _____
2. eenlde _____
3. lipl _____
4. lubamcean _____
5. rootcd _____
6. heaclriwhe _____
7. deb nap _____
8. gednaba _____
9. decimnie _____
10. tacs _____
11. tememhreotr _____
12. dolob _____

1. nurse
2. needle
3. pill
4. ambulance
5. doctor
6. wheelchair
7. bed pan
8. bandage
9. medicine
10. cast
11. thermometer
12. blood

77

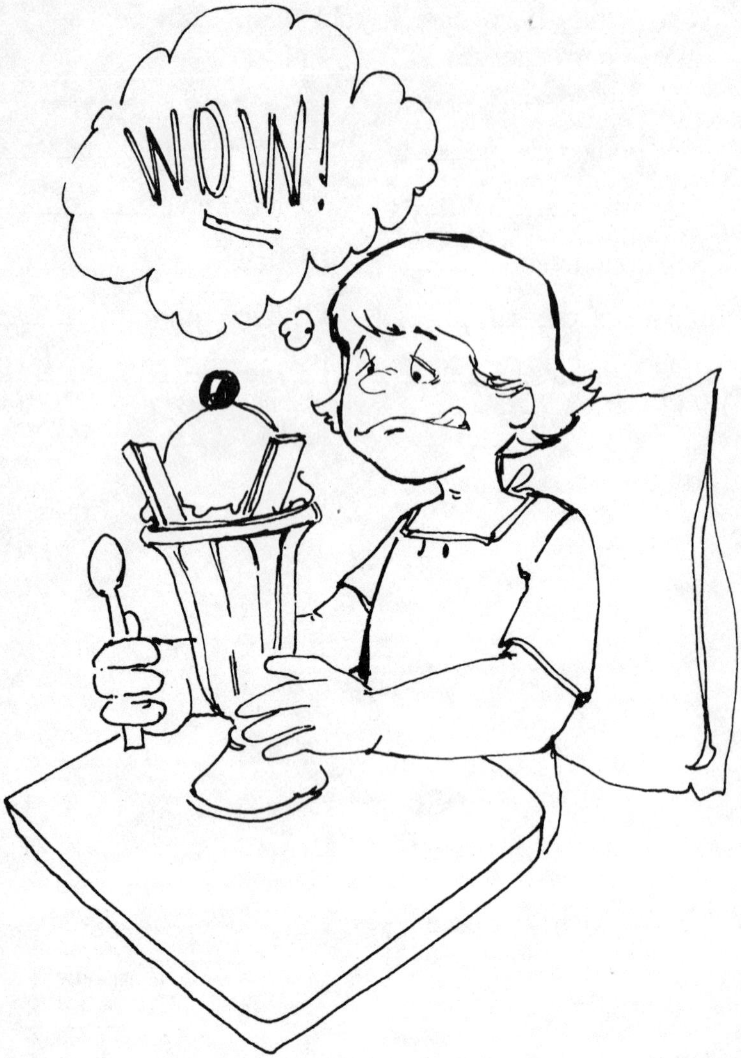
WOW!

Good-bye, Tonsils; Hello, Ice Cream!

Has the doctor decided you need to have your tonsils removed? Maybe you were having sore throats or your hearing wasn't as good as usual. Before even more serious problems arise, it would be better to get rid of those tonsils.

Doctors believe the general purpose of tonsils is to fight germs in the body. If the tonsils become infected, they not only can't do their job, but they begin to work against the person.

Medicine is tried first. However, when the tonsils are in too bad condition, they must be taken out.

Actually you have several sets of tonsils. The most common are the *palatine* tonsils in the back of the mouth. There are also the *lingual* tonsils on the back of the tongue. Another is the *pharyngeal* tonsil (often called adenoids), located at the back of the nose.

Don't be fooled. The skin you see hanging from the roof of your mouth is not your tonsils. This is the uvula.

An infected tonsil is called tonsillitis. The removal of the tonsil is a tonsillectomy. Generally this is a simple surgery. Many adults are given shots to numb the area and are not even put to sleep. Children are almost always given a general anesthetic so they will be slumbering.

Every operation is serious but this type of surgery is

one of the easiest. If everything goes well, the patient will go home the day after the tonsillectomy.

While the patient's throat is sore, he or she has to eat soft foods. This is your chance to order plenty of ice cream! Within a few days you should feel better than ever and be fully active again.

Don't forget to take a few notes so you can remember the facts.

1. Which set of my tonsils are going to be removed? (Ask the nurse or doctor.)
   _____

2. How many days do I expect to be in the hospital?
   _____

3. Did I get ice cream? _____ What kind? _____
4. How did my throat feel after the operation? _____
   _____

5. What do doctors call the removal of the tonsils? _____
   _____

6. How many people have I met in the hospital who are having their tonsils taken out? _____
   What are the names of two of them? _____
   _____

7. Has my nurse had her tonsils taken out? _____

There Goes Your Appendix!

If you are in the hospital for an appendix operation, you are fortunate. Some children don't get to the hospital in time and their appendix bursts. When this happens their insides become covered with bacteria and they are in big trouble.

This operation is called an "appendectomy." One out of every ten children has his appendix removed. It is done so often by so many doctors that you can expect things to go smoothly.

How did you know you had appendix trouble or "appendicitis"? Was there a pain in your side? Usually there is a fever; this is caused by infection in your system.

Your appendix is normally about the size of a small finger. When it becomes inflamed it puffs up like a balloon. This is why it is so painful to the touch.

The operation will not take long. After you are put to sleep the doctor will make an incision into your side. You won't feel a thing. You can keep on counting race cars or buying clothes in your sleep.

It will take the doctor only a minute to find your appendix in your intestine. When his rubber-gloved hands locate it, he will merely give it a quick snip with his tiny, sterilized scissors.

The doctor will sew the intestine, then put it back in place. He will then sew stitches into your side to close the incision.

Your body will work just fine without the appendix.

When the doctor is finished, you will probably be taken to a recovery room. Here nurses will watch you closely until you wake up.

Don't be surprised if you feel terrible when you first open your eyes. You might feel dizzy and your stomach may feel sick. You will probaby start to wake up and fall back to sleep. This could happen several times. That's normal.

Gradually you will start to feel stronger and eat better. In a few days you should be on your way home.

How Did You Like Your Adventure?

Now that you're home, write down your feelings about the hospital.

1. What is life really like in a hospital? _____
   _____

2. What was the best part about being in the hospital?
   _____

3. What was the hardest part? _____
   _____

4. What did I find that I didn't expect? _____
   _____

5. What would I change about hospitals? _____
   _____

6. If I worked in a hospital, what job would I most like? Why? _____
   _____
   _____

Autographs of Other Patients I Met

Autographs of Relatives and Friends Who Visited Me

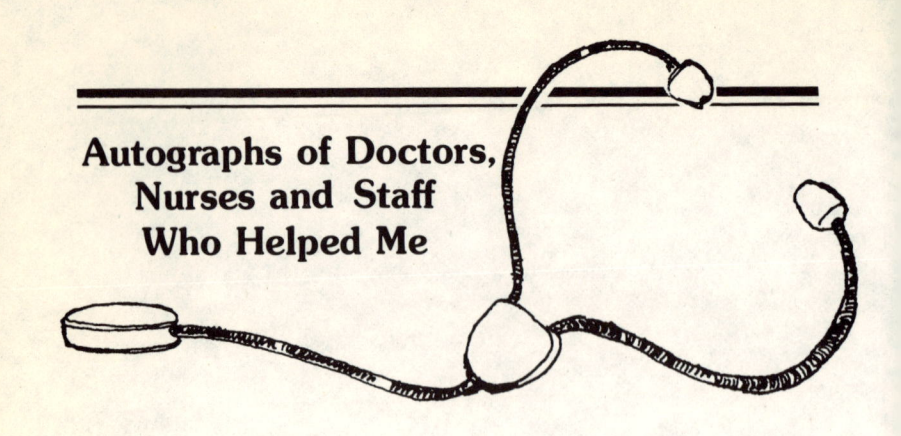

**Autographs of Doctors,
Nurses and Staff
Who Helped Me**

A Summary of My Hospital Stay

(Use these pages to draw pictures or write stories about your hospital stay.)

Devotionals for families with young children by William L. Coleman

Counting Stars, meditations on God's creation.

My Magnificent Machine, devotionals centered around the marvels of the human body.

Listen to the Animals, lessons from the animal world.

On Your Mark, challenges from the lives of well-known athletes.

The Good Night Book, bedtime inspirationals (especially for those who may be afraid of the dark).

More About My Magnificent Machine, more devotionals describing parts of the human body and how they reflect the genius of the Creator.

Today I Feel Like a Warm Fuzzy, devotionals for small children which help them to identify and learn how to respond to their own feelings and emotions.

Singing Penguins and Puffed-Up Toads, fifty-two underwater adventures for family devotions.

Chesapeake Charlie Series

Chesapeake Charlie mystery/adventure stories are for ages 10-14.

Chesapeake Charlie and the Bay Bank Robbers
Chesapeake Charlie and Blackbeard's Treasure
Chesapeake Charlie and the Stolen Diamond